An Autobiography of
the Autobiography
of Reading

DIONNE BRAND

An Autobiography of
the Autobiography
of Reading

CLC KREISEL LECTURE SERIES

Canadian Literature Centre
Centre de littérature canadienne

UNIVERSITY *of* ALBERTA PRESS

Published by

University of Alberta Press
1-16 Rutherford Library South
11204 89 Avenue NW
Edmonton, Alberta, Canada   T6G 2J4
uap.ualberta.ca
and
Canadian Literature Centre /
Centre de littérature canadienne
3-5 Humanities Centre
University of Alberta
Edmonton, Alberta, Canada   T6G 2E5
abclc.ca

LIBRARY AND ARCHIVES CANADA
CATALOGUING IN PUBLICATION

Title: An autobiography of the
    autobiography of reading / Dionne
    Brand.
Names: Brand, Dionne, 1953- author.
Series: Henry Kreisel lecture series.
Description: Series statement: CLC Kreisel
    lecture series | Includes bibliographical
    references.
Identifiers: Canadiana (print) 20190217243 |
    Canadiana (ebook) 20190217251 |
    ISBN 9781772125085 (softcover) |
    ISBN 9781772125139 (EPUB) |
    ISBN 9781772125146 (Kindle) |
    ISBN 9781772125153 (PDF)
Subjects: LCSH: Brand, Dionne, 1953- —
    Books and reading. | LCSH: Blacks
    in literature. | LCSH: Imperialism
    in literature. | LCSH: Colonies in
    literature. | LCSH: Racism in literature. |
    LCSH: Authorship.
Classification: LCC PS8553.R275 Z46 2020 |
    DDC C811/.54—dc23

First edition, first printing, 2020.
First printed and bound in Canada
by Houghton Boston Printers,
Saskatoon, Saskatchewan.
Copyediting and proofreading by
Joanne Muzak.

The Canadian Literature Centre
acknowledges the support of Dr. Eric
Schloss and the Faculty of Arts for the CLC
Kreisel Lecture delivered by Dionne Brand
in April 2019 at the University of Alberta.

University of Alberta Press gratefully
acknowledges the support received for its
publishing program from the Government
of Canada, the Canada Council for the Arts,
and the Government of Alberta through the
Alberta Media Fund.

FOREWORD

The CLC Kreisel Lecture Series

THE CLC KREISEL LECTURES bring together writers, readers, students, scholars, teachers—and with this book, publisher and research centre—in an open, inclusive, and critical literary forum. The series has also fostered a beautiful partnership between the CLC and CBC Radio 1 *Ideas*, which has produced exciting broadcasts that feature the lecturers themselves—including Michael Crummey, Heather O'Neill, Margaret Atwood, and Lynn Coady— and further probe each lecture's themes. Through this partnership, the Kreisel Lectures are able to reach an audience of over a million listeners. The Kreisel Series raises a myriad of issues, at times painful, at times joyful, but always salient and far-reaching: oppression and social justice, cultural identity, place and displacement, the spoils of history, storytelling, censorship, language, reading in a digital age, literary history, and personal memory. The Kreisel Series confronts topics that concern us all within the specificities of our contemporary experience, whatever our differences. In the spirit of free and honest dialogue, it does so with thoughtfulness and depth as well as humour and grace.

These public lectures also set out to honour Professor Henry Kreisel's legacy in an annual public forum. Author, University Professor, and Officer of the Order of Canada, Henry Kreisel was born in Vienna into a Jewish family in 1922. He left his homeland for England in 1938 and was interned, in Canada, for eighteen months during the Second World War. After studying at the University of Toronto, he began teaching in 1947 at the University of Alberta, and served as Chair of English from 1961 until 1970. He served as Vice-President (Academic) from 1970 to 1975, and was named University Professor in 1975, the highest scholarly award bestowed on its faculty members by the University of Alberta. Professor Kreisel was an inspiring and beloved teacher who taught generations of students to love literature and was one of the first people to bring the experience of the immigrant to modern Canadian literature. He died in Edmonton in 1991. His works include two novels, *The Rich Man* (1948) and *The Betrayal* (1964), and a collection of short stories, *The Almost Meeting* (1981). His internment diary, alongside critical essays on his writing, appears in *Another Country: Writings by and about Henry Kreisel* (1985).

The generosity of Professor Kreisel's teaching at the University of Alberta profoundly inspires the CLC in its public outreach, research pursuits, and continued commitment to the ever-growing richness, complexity, and diversity of Canada's writings. The Centre embraces Henry Kreisel's pioneering focus on the knowledge of one's own literatures. It is in his memory that we seek to foster a better understanding of a difficult world, which literature can help us reimagine and even transform.

The Canadian Literature Centre was established in 2006, thanks to the leadership gift of the noted Edmontonian bibliophile, Dr. Eric Schloss.

MARIE CARRIÈRE

Director, Canadian Literature Centre

Edmonton, May 2019

LIMINAIRE

La Collection des Conférences Kreisel du CLC

LES CONFÉRENCES KREISEL DU CLC rassemblent
écrivains et écrivaines, lecteurs et lectrices, étudiants
et étudiantes, chercheurs et chercheuses, enseignants
et enseignantes—éditeur et centre de recherche grâce
à ce livre—dans un forum littéraire ouvert, inclusif et
critique. La collection entretient aussi un magnifique
partenariat entre le CLC et CBC Radio 1 « Ideas » dont
les radiodiffusions mettent en vedette les conférenciers
et conférencières—y compris Michael Crummey, Heather
O'Neill, Margaret Atwood et Lynn Coady—interrogeant
de plus près les thèmes de leur conférence pour un public
de plus d'un million. La Collection Kreisel met en valeur
de nombreuses problématiques, parfois douloureuses,
parfois joyeuses, or toujours saillantes et considérables:
oppression et justice sociale, identité culturelle, lieu et
déplacement, dépouilles de l'histoire, narration, censure,
langage, lecture à l'ère numérique, histoire littéraire et
mémoire personnelle. La Collection Kreisel s'affronte aux
questions qui nous concernent tous et toutes selon les
spécificités de notre vécu contemporain, peu important
nos différences. Dans une intention de dialogue libre et

honnête, elle se produit dans l'ardeur et la profondeur intellectuelles ainsi que l'humour et l'élégance.

Ces conférences publiques et annuelles se consacrent à perpétuer la mémoire du Professeur Henry Kreisel. Auteur, professeur universitaire et Officier de l'Ordre du Canada, Henry Kreisel est né à Vienne d'une famille juive en 1922. En 1938, il a quitté son pays natal pour l'Angleterre et a été interné pendant dix-huit mois, au Canada, lors de la Deuxième Guerre mondiale. Après ses études à l'Université de Toronto, il devint professeur à l'Université de l'Alberta en 1947, et à partir de 1961 jusqu'à 1970, il a dirigé le Département d'anglais. De 1970 à 1975, il a été vice-recteur (universitaire), et a été nommé professeur hors rang en 1975, la plus haute distinction scientifique décernée par l'Université de l'Alberta à un membre de son professorat. Professeur adoré, il a transmis l'amour de la littérature à plusieurs générations d'étudiants, et il a été parmi les premiers écrivains modernes du Canada à aborder l'expérience immigrante. Il est décédé à Edmonton en 1991. Son œuvre comprend les romans, *The Rich Man* (1948) et *The Betrayal* (1964), et un recueil de nouvelles intitulé *The Almost Meeting* (1981). Son journal d'internement, accompagné d'articles critiques sur ses écrits, paraît dans *Another Country: Writings by and about Henry Kreisel* (1985).

La générosité du Professeur Kreisel est une source d'inspiration profonde quant au travail public et scientifique du CLC de sonder la grande diversité, complexité et qualité remarquable des écrits du Canada. Le Centre adhère à l'importance qu'accordait de façon inaugurale Henry Kreisel à la connaissance des littératures de son propre pays. C'est à sa mémoire que nous poursuivons une meilleure compréhension d'un monde difficile que la littérature peut nous aider à imaginer et transformer.

Le Centre de littérature canadienne a été créé en 2006 grâce au don directeur du bibliophile illustre edmontonien, le docteur Eric Schloss.

MARIE CARRIÈRE

Directrice, Centre de littérature canadienne

Edmonton, mai 2019

THERE IS A PHOTOGRAPH of me taken when I was a child. I do not recognize myself, though I seem to remember the day and the event. The little girl, reputed to be me, in the photograph is about three or four years old. It is the earliest and only photograph of this period. They say that I am one of the four children in this photograph; the three others are my sisters and my closest cousin. I recognize *them*. We are four girls. I am alleged to be second from the left, third from the right. We all have white ribbons in our hair. We are taking a photograph to send to England to my mother and her younger sister, who are in England becoming nurses. Several years before, they had left by boat, by ship, perhaps a Cunard ship, whose name my aunt does not recall now, though she does recall passing Tenerife, standing on deck—thinking that one day she would like to go back there. She says this with the same longing as then. They arrived at the port of Southampton, my aunt and my mother, sometime in 1956. From Southampton they took a boat-train to London, where they were gathered by the hospital they were assigned to. This boat-train I meet later in the wonderful first sentence of Samuel Selvon's novel *The Lonely Londoners*:

> One grim winter evening, when it had a kind of
> unrealness about London, with a fog sleeping restlessly
> over the city and the lights showing in the blur as if is not
> London at all but some strange place on another planet,
> Moses Aloetta hop on a number 46 bus at the corner of
> Chepstow Road and Westbourne Grove to go to Waterloo
> to meet a fellar who was coming from Trinidad on the
> boat-train.[1]

I imagine that my mother and my aunt encounter this
same London as described by Selvon. When we take
the photograph, we are taking it to send to my mother
and my aunt, but also to send to England. England is
in the air at home. It is referred to with reverence as
"away" or "abroad." England is as much the spectator;
and for England, standing behind my mother and my
aunt, we must make a good appearance. They arrived
in London under the impression that they, too, had to
make a good appearance, so that they and we would be
accepted and acceptable. I am, to my mind, the most
active in the photograph, helping the photographer to
make the photograph right. I remember my younger
sister and cousin crying and the photographer, Mr. Wong,
assigning me to distract them with a toy rattle. I take
my job seriously. Now, it seems mechanically. My mother
and my aunt have left under the impression that they,
too, must make a good appearance. We must look out
into the camera, Mr. Wong says, "Little girls, smile! Don't
cry." I recall trying to follow his instruction; my little
sister is crying, and my cousin is trembling in sympathy.
My older sister is aloof with her own self-arrangement.
I remember all of these actions, but I do not recognize

the girl who is me in the photograph. Whoever I appear to be is simply that: an appearance. As when you come upon a figure across a street in a glass-walled building. Yet even more remote than this. I cannot even make out a gestural similarity. Except for my older sister, we three youngest do not remember my mother and my aunt. We only know of them from stories, from the frequent invocation of their names in the house where we live. My mother and my aunt are in the imagination and so, too, is England, where they now live and where they are said to be getting along. We are all tied to England, and England to the imagination. All letters after—all communication of information, endearment, and entreaty—will go to and arrive from Wandle Valley Hospital, Mitcham Junction, Surrey, England. Sixty years later my older sister will still remember this address by heart. And all the letters, back and forth, will begin with this courtesy: *Dear* _____, *Hope you are well and enjoying the best of health.* England will be the recipient, the audience. England is a better place. Our lives will revolve around and be decided in the letters sent and received.

Everyone says the little girl looks like me. I doubt it. I do not recognize myself. Already I am changed in the photograph, since I leave off being myself to follow the directive of the photographer; already I have changed, thinking of composing myself, for the audience. I now recognize myself as authored, altered. As selected, sorted, from a series of selves for appearance and presentation. All photographs are like this, of course. One is conscious or anxious or confident or deliberate in striking an appearance that must keep, must transmit one's meaning— or the photographer's meaning. That is the studium, as

Barthes describes in *Camera Lucida*—and that photograph
is supposed to reach its viewers and reassure them. And
it probably does. Though we, we are without conscious
meaning, which is why we are crying or aloof or attentive
to the photographer—and that is the punctum. The
photograph or the job the photographer must do is
disrupted by the indecorousness of some of the subjects,
the disparate attitudes of the little girls who, despite
being told of the importance and expense of the occasion
of the photograph, respond in wholly individual ways.
They do not even mean to disrupt; they have been warned
not to be ill-behaved, as I recall. But they've panicked
in the face of these disciplines. The stranger who is the
photographer, the new linoleum smell of the room where
the photograph is being taken, the tripod, the camera, the
warning to behave, and the shy desire to have themselves
be seen by the mother and the aunt in England.
Ultimately, the photograph can't do all the work it is
required to do—the photograph does produce them—but
they are in the middle of being something—still pliable,
permeable—you can see all that in the photograph—and
that disrupts the work the photo is being sent out to
do—they are/we are not properly composed. The photo
also perhaps confirms the disciplining work to be done.
Despite Mr. Wong's arrangement of us by height, despite
his angles and the curtain behind and the linoleum floor
composition, the photo cannot hold the girls in. And
perhaps we will remain in this liminal space between
photograph and meaning—permeable. But perhaps not.

The permeability evident in the photograph will
yield to instruction from here on—instruction that also
arrives from English schoolbooks, English academic

testing, English literature that a colonial apparatus provides. I will go on to Miss Greenidge's Dame School, I will go on to the San Fernando Girls English Catholic School, I will go on to the Naparima Girls' High School, sending letters and receiving instructions from England; from Surrey, then from Croyden, then from "Pip and the Convict," "Dick Whittington and His Cat," "Bobby Shafto's Gone to Sea," "To a Butterfly," "Oh Mary, go and call the cattle home...across the sands o'Dee"—becoming, becoming the representation of the self, signified by the opportunity of the photographic event.

A photograph. A portrait, desired, settled, and puncturing the frame of the photograph. All the relations that come together to make the portrait—the children, the mother, and the aunt waiting for the photograph, the adult outside of the frame who brought the children here to take the photograph, the photographer, who has taken many such photographs to send to mothers and aunts and fathers and sisters—England, observing these children over the shoulders of mothers and aunts. This porous portrait is full of multiple autobiographies: Mr. Wong, the photographer, probably traces his family to Chinese indentured labour—1846 or perhaps even as far back as 1806 (Indian indentured labour beginning in 1845 also makes up the historical in the town where the photography studio operates); the children, their history goes back to the period of Arawak/Carib extermination and the enslavement and transportation of their families from West Africa to the New World. They meet in a photography studio some hundred and odd years later to all follow a custom marked at every step with colonial imperative. All of these violent trajectories have been synthesized in the photograph. The act of taking the photograph is deeply calculated to "arrive," to align with the imperative. It is an attempt to "appear," to synchronize with coloniality's time of modernity, of proper subjectivity.

I call this essay "An Autobiography of the Autobiography of Reading," leading with the indefinite *An Autobiography*, which leaves open the possibility of multiple autobiographies, that this is but one iteration; it is particular but not individual. An autobiography gestures to the world of a reading self. It signals the complicated ways of reading and interpretation that are necessary under conditions of coloniality. It suggests that coloniality constructs outsides and insides—worlds to be chosen, disturbed, interpreted, and navigated—in order to live something like a real self. The definite article of the second clause *the Autobiography* identifies the subject who is supposed to be made, through colonial pedagogies in the form of texts—fiction, non-fiction, poetry, photographs, and governmental and bureaucratic structures. This subject situated at the meeting of violent pasts and futures of coloniality is hailed ambiguously in these texts to simultaneously be mastered and elide to mastery as something other than violence, erasure, and absence.

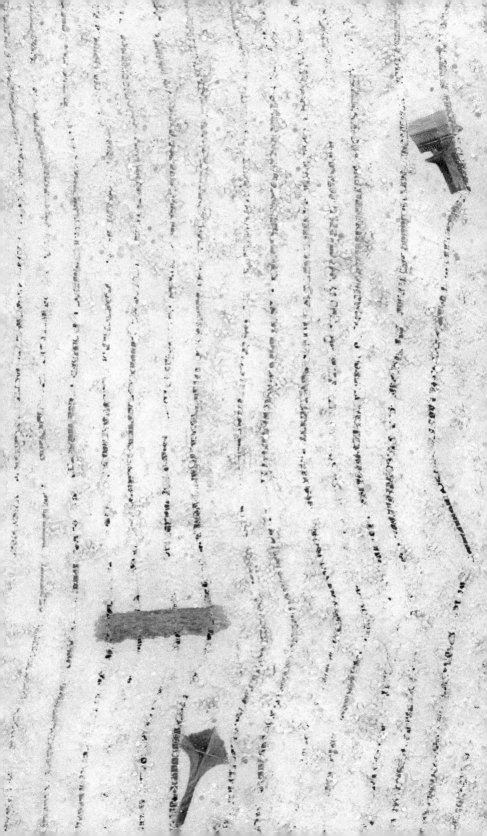

THE GREAT POLYMATH—historian, novelist, critic, and political scientist—C.L.R. James begins that majestic book *Beyond a Boundary* with a chapter called "The Window." In it he describes the window of his childhood house at the turn into the twentieth century—through this window he could see the cricket pitch of the town of Tunapuna. There, standing on a chair at six years old, he spent many Saturday hours watching men practise the art of cricket. He also describes a childhood of reading incessantly and in particular William Thackeray's *Vanity Fair*. In *Beyond a Boundary*, James writes, "Thackeray, not Marx, bears the heaviest responsibility for me."[2] *Thackeray, not Marx, bears the heaviest responsibility for me.* Scholars have gone over these lines of James's with varying interpretations. Among these interpretations is that James was throwing shade on Marx, but if one reads the sentences before that one, one might approximate a truer answer. "I laughed without satiety at Thackeray's constant jokes and sneers and gibes at the aristocracy and at people in high places."[3] Here, James credits Thackeray with exposing the hypocrisy of the nineteenth-century British aristocracy. James is responding with the alternate knowledge of a man historically on the other side of that aristocracy. James continues, "But the things I did not notice and took for granted were more enduring: the British reticence, the British self-discipline, the stiff lips, upper and lower. When Major Dobbin returns from India, and he and Amelia greet each other, Thackeray asks: Why did Dobbin not speak?...George Osborne writes a cold, stiff letter to his estranged father before going into battle, but he places a kiss on the envelope which Thackeray notes that his father did not see."[4] Here, James points to the British mores promulgated at the time, mores that were to become tropes in the national consciousness, tropes that James was inculcated in despite their glaring contradictions. Then the passages about colonial teaching practices in the colonized world: "Not only the English masters, but Englishmen in their relation to games in the colonies held tightly to the code as example and as a mark of differentiation."[5] And the ways in which those codes of coloniality lay contradictorily and harshly in the colonized. "I was an actor on a stage in which the parts were set in advance. I not only took it to an extreme, I seemed to have been made by nature for nothing else. There were others around me who did not go as far and as completely as I did."[6]

James's *Beyond a Boundary* analyzes the game of cricket in order to set out the terms of coloniality laid down by the British and the acquisition and demolition of those terms by West Indies cricket of the 1940s, '50s, and '60s:

> In the West Indies the cricket ethic has shaped not
> only the cricketers but social life as a whole. It is an
> understatement. There is a whole generation of us, and

perhaps two generations, who have been formed by it not only in social attitudes but in our most intimate personal lives, in fact there more than anywhere else. The social attitudes we could to some degree alter if we wished. For the inner self the die was cast...Along with restraint, not so much externally as in internal inhibitions, we learnt loyalty. It is good to be loyal to what you believe in—that, however, may be tautology. Loyalty to what is wrong, outmoded, reactionary is mischievous. To that in general all will agree, even the reactionary.[7]

Lisa Lowe, in *The Intimacies of Four Continents*, interprets James's formulation—that Thackeray, not Marx, made him—as James's appreciation of the way the novel describes the history of global empire. She writes:

> *Literature and culture mediated these early nineteenth-century world conditions, not by literally reflecting them in a fixed, transparent fashion, but rather by thematizing the manners in which imperial culture simultaneously recognized yet suppressed the emerging contradictions of the era...Literature mediates these asymmetries of dominant, residual, and emergent forces, inasmuch as it may portray that such conditions were more often grasped as isolated effects, glimpsed in particular objects in the social fabric, rather than seized totally or framed systematically.*[8]

Perhaps Thackeray, not Marx, made me too. Made and unmade. But perhaps, more importantly, James made me. His book on the Haitian revolution, *The Black Jacobins: Toussaint L'Ouverture and the San Domingo Revolution*; his novel *Minty Alley*; his political theory *Notes on Dialectics*. And when I read those lines of James in *Beyond a Boundary*, the elegant work on cricket and literature and politics, they took me back to my own childhood and first reading of *Vanity Fair*—back to Amelia Sedley, Becky Sharpe, William Dobbin, Rawdon Crawley, George Osborne. Like James, I read *Vanity Fair* first at a young age, perhaps twelve, and then in my twenties in a nineteenth-century literature class at university. The memory of my childhood reading brings *not* lessons in restraint and the code of masculinity, or inhibition, or the great sprawl of colonial domination, that last colonial domination (at least not on the surface), although ingested as the acceptable and inevitable, the fabric of social hierarchies, the material world itself. But that memory summoned the codes and lessons of femininity. Amelia Sedley's and Becky Sharpe's thrown into stark moral relief—Amelia: gentle, rosy-cheeked smiling, pliant, and good; Becky: cunning, ungrateful, bitter, and destined for no good. The narrative summoned me to attend to the example of Amelia Sedley, innocent and unconscious of the world, and therefore safe. And Becky Sharpe, too worldly, too clever, too grasping, too knowledgeable, and therefore doomed. I was with Amelia, wanting her to be happy, wanting her to have Osborne, wanting Dobbin to take care of her. Why couldn't Becky *behave?*

For as Thackeray himself says later:

> Miss Sedley (*whom we have selected for the very reason that she was the best-natured of all, otherwise what on earth was to have prevented us from putting up Miss Swartz, or Miss Crump, or Miss Hopkins, as heroine in*

her place?) it could not be expected that every one should
be of the humble and gentle temper of Miss Amelia Sedley;
should take every opportunity to vanquish Rebecca's
hard-heartedness and ill-humour; and, by a thousand
kind words and offices, overcome, for once at least, her
hostility to her kind.[9]

The obvious parody of femininity notwithstanding,
because, after all, the outcome/alternative is unavailable
in the text, I was called to choose. Then there was another
figure, who appears on page 7 of *Vanity Fair*: "Miss Swartz,
the rich woolly-haired mulatto from St. Kitt's."[10] But
I barely remembered her and only found her again as
a stunning surprise on rereading. Thackeray also had a
drawing of Miss Swartz, a drawing I must have decidedly
forgotten or clinically forgotten, since to me, it was
such a horrific drawing of a Black woman seemingly
uncomfortable in cosquelle Victorian wear. Reading
narrative requires, demands, acts of identification,
association, affiliation, sympathy, and empathy, acts of
en/inhabiting. And while James associated with and
inhabited the faithful, loyal, and restrained Dobbin, the
heroic George Osborne, I inhabited the good, kind, gentle,
somewhat insipid Amelia. (You must remember that
"insipid" is one of the categories of femininity.) The
geopolitics of empire had already prepared me for this
identification as it had prepared James—the goods,
information, the structures of bureaucracy, the physical
colonial layout of place attenuating location, the systems
of education in schools, language, manners—the hierarchies
were already set out and therefore so were the ambitions.
Or, at least I was invited to inhabit Amelia by the mere

presentation of her as innocence and goodness, silence, inaction, and vapidity as "character" in the text.

But how did I miss Miss Swartz? Why did I not enter Miss Swartz? Yes, she was not the main protagonist, but why did I forget Miss Swartz? And why on several readings was Miss Swartz always a surprise to me? A shock that took me away from, that disturbed, the narrative and that threatened to impede. And how, how did I miss on the very first page of *Vanity Fair* another figure, how did I read right by him? He was, after all, the furniture, the opening mechanism for transporting all of Thackeray's text. And, of course, *Vanity Fair* is a parody, a critique of aristocratic Britain during this phase of imperialism. But even in a critique and parody, blackness is doubly parodied. Because blackness is parody. So how did I miss Sambo? On the first page! What slippage of interpretation accomplished that? Why did I notice him only with dismayed recognition after years of decompression out of imperialist aesthetic? Did I miss him or take him, and Miss Swartz, for granted, did I swallow them as the indigestible but necessary meal of coloniality on the way, nevertheless, to occupying and identifying with the colonial? For the text to work on this reader the way that it is supposed to, I cannot see her, I cannot remember her or Sambo. She, they, had to remain a perpetual surprise. Like the surprise of seeing myself that is not myself. I must have recognized her with disappointment as the representation of me, the stand-in for blackness and all its significations, and even as a child I understood them both to be without future in the narrative, and subject to horrifying sanctions.

Back to *Vanity Fair*. Here is Sambo on the first page:

> *While the present century was in its teens, and on one
> sun-shiny morning in June, there drove up to the great
> iron gate of Miss Pinkerton's academy for young ladies,
> on Chiswick Mall, a large family coach, with two fat
> horses in blazing harness, driven by a fat coachman in
> a three-cornered hat and wig, at the rate of four miles
> an hour. A black servant, who reposed on the box beside
> the fat coachman, uncurled his bandy legs as soon as
> the equipage drew up opposite Miss Pinkerton's shining
> brass plate, and as he pulled the bell... "It is Mrs. Sedley's
> coach, sister," said Miss Jemima. "Sambo, the black
> servant, has just rung the bell; and the coachman has a
> new red waistcoat."*[11]

How did I, on first reading, miss them? Or did I? Miss
Swartz is mentioned thirty-six times. Her wealth as the
daughter of a planter (who we are told is Jewish and an
undesignated Black woman—read *enslaved*) does see
her married to aristocracy eventually, and throughout
Thackeray makes great play of her without suggesting
what particular quality of her we must make play, leaving
us to (arrive, as if on our own at) race as the laughable
quality. Both Sambo and Miss Swartz are figures of the
comic. The comic appears to position them diametrically
to their actual importance to the text's economic
obligations. Another figure, Loll Jewab, an Indian man
who is a servant, is variously described as mistaken for
the devil or having yellow eyes and white teeth—a farcical
dismissal of India's importance to the colonial project.

The names themselves are caricatures.

Thackeray's narrative schema, his arrangement of elements of action, requires and places these figures as settled. Our reading and writing practices too—reading and writing as practices located within the ways we live and imagine ourselves in the world—admit and require the schema. We are as curious about them as we are about a necessary bit of denotative furniture described. They enrich the text in crucial ways, but they do not live. Thackeray, after all, is writing this text in 1847; he is aware of his time, referring to the avarice without condemning or addressing slavery, the slave trade, the exploitation of India and China. The mores of the British aristocracy are his main concerns, not colonial exploitation. And the novel is a scathing indictment of those mores, but nowhere does it indict what that wealth is built on. Thackeray was born in India, his father a secretary of the East India Company.

Edward Said writes in *Culture and Imperialism*:

> Nearly everywhere in nineteenth- and early-twentieth-century British and French culture we find allusions to the facts of empire, but perhaps nowhere with more regularity and frequency than in the British novel. Taken together, these allusions constitute what I have called a structure of attitude and reference.[12]

I want to say that, perhaps more than *allusion* or *reference*, my point is that these are embedded in the production of form of the novel and structure of feeling intended to be produced by the novel. Everyone, meaning individuals and corporations, had their hands in slavery and colonial exploitation, just as today they have their hands in oil or minerals and electronics as they destroy the earth on which we live, the oceans, the air, and say it is about jobs and our livelihoods.

So, I am talking about what sits in narrative as a result of the genesis, the action and long duration, of certain regimes in our material lives, certain relations of power, so as to make invisible or ordinary, or a given, those power relations. And I am talking about how those power relations are embedded in narrative.

James would have seen this as I did later: the aristocracy flush with money, their fortunes flowing; the Napoleonic Wars' deep effects on control of territories in the New World; colonial conquest embedded in the book without any of the actors from those places speaking, only appearing as fixed. The action of *Vanity Fair* takes place during British slavery. (The writing of the novel takes place shortly after abolition.) Slavery is never mentioned in the text, but virtue, modesty, goodness, and religion and god are. So, there is a society proceeding as if these things are divisible from enslavement. Conquest gives the narrative its velocity and moral reasoning—but it is the welfare of the conquerors that is at stake. Parody never undermines them.

For me, of course, the whole novel is immersed in slavery. Thackeray may be talking about the superficiality of class and gender, but for me it is the glassy surface, a mirrored surface of violent narrative that one is watching and inhabiting and underneath is the pedagogy of colony. While class and gender (the making of white class, white gender) may have been the obvious subjects of the narrative, race and colony as bedrocks of power are startlingly unremarked; in fact, normalized, stipulated, matter-of-fact.

The constant reinforcement of the unseen, unread, the hardening of narrative position, is the pedagogy of colony.

Which brings me to Thackeray's *The History of Henry Esmond, Esq.* An historical novel of the life of Henry Esmond, it was published in 1852. The time of the novel is the early 1700s. For my purposes, it is not important what the story is. I want to look at the language—what it transmits, the state of being it describes, the mind, the philosophical orientation of the speaker. I want to look at the language, in this case, English, as vehicular—as transporting ideas of the normal at the level of syntax and feeling; as marking the relation of objects.

The History of Henry Esmond, Esq. begins:

> *The estate of Castlewood, in Virginia, which was given to our ancestors by King Charles the First, as some return for the sacrifices made in His Majesty's cause by the Esmond family, lies in Westmoreland county, between the rivers Potomac and Rappahannoc, and was once as great as an English Principality, though in the early times its revenues were but small. Indeed for near eighty years after our forefathers possessed them, our plantations were in the hands of factors, who enriched themselves one after another, though a few scores of hogsheads of tobacco were all the produce, that, for long after the Restoration, our family received from their Virginian estates.*[13]

Notice the tenor of the paragraph, the relational claims it makes, the elevated stance of the speaker. Notice the emotive words it deploys—*returns for the sacrifices, given to our ancestors, our forefathers possessed.* Note the invocation of the King, the words *great as an English Principality,* then the gesture to the wrongfully disadvantaged state of the family. All these words go to invoking regard and sympathy and summoning association. To read this first paragraph is to read two worlds: the world being addressed and the world buried in the address. So, let us look at other words in the text, their deployment and their effects: *Potomac and Rappahannoc, our plantations, factors, hogsheads of tobacco.* This language is of objects relating to the inanimate or in the case of *factors* two senses, figure/sums, and advantage. But what do I read from *Potomac and Rappahannoc* but Indigeneity and previous habitation—old habitation if something like the name of a river is resistant to an English principality; and in *plantations*—forced labour/enslavement of Black people, after all we are in Virginia, that labour exploited to produce hogsheads of tobacco. Suddenly my reading is populated by a force of Black people unmentioned, moving about, living, and it is populated by their suffering. A set of exploitative relations comes into focus in this now. But the vehicular language suspends the meanings of this exploitation and human suffering and replaces them with a dreary tale of white disenfranchisement.

In his essay "Aesthetic Reflection and the Colonial Event: The Work of Art in the Age of Slavery," Simon Gikandi writes:

> *First, colonial events and subjects are never centered in the European discourse on the aesthetic, which dominates the 18th century, but they occupy important footnotes*

> or addenda; if the aesthetic acquires its ideal character
> by its force of exclusion...it is, nevertheless, haunted by
> that which it excludes...Since the end of the 18th century,
> debates about the aesthetic...[have been] concerned with
> the nature and judgement of beauty and explanation
> of artistic phenomena—and unconcerned with the
> turbulence associated with the colonial empire.[14]

From The History of Henry Esmond, Esq. again:

> Neither my father nor my mother ever wore powder in
> their hair; both their heads were as white as silver, as
> I can remember them. My dear mother possessed to
> the last an extraordinary brightness and freshness of
> complexion; nor would people believe that she did not
> wear rouge. At sixty years of age she still looked young,
> and was quite agile. It was not until after that dreadful
> siege of our house by the Indians, which left me a widow
> ere I was a mother, that my dear mother's health broke.
> She never recovered from her terror and anxiety of those
> days, which ended so fatally for me, then a bride scarce
> six months married, and died in my father's arms ere
> my own year of widowhood was over.[15]

I have to admit reading this with cold-bloodedness,
or at least I cannot do what the reader is hailed to do,
which is to juxtapose the refinement, good taste, beauty,
and rectitude of the mother, ergo England, against the
dreadful siege and terror of the Indians. The reader
occupying the autobiography of reading. Instead, I admit
to laughter and satisfaction at this siege and the early

decease of the mother. That I say I *have to admit* and
call myself cold-blooded, and I admit to laughter as if
it isn't warranted, speaks to the presumption that the
vehicular language has transported the pathos to the
correct subject and that I am that reading subject who
must respond to the material transported—namely,
identification with the protagonist and some moral tenet,
some tenet of proper aesthetic appreciation.

Thackeray's *The History of Henry Esmond, Esq.* begins
with the conceit of a preface from Esmond's daughter:

> *Though I never heard my father use a rough word, 'twas*
> *extraordinary with how much awe his people regarded*
> *him; and the servants on our plantation, both those*
> *assigned from England and the purchased negroes,*
> *obeyed him with an eagerness such as the most severe*
> *taskmasters round about us could never get from their*
> *people. He was never familiar, though perfectly simple*
> *and natural; he was the same with the meanest man as*
> *with the greatest, and as courteous to a black slave-girl*
> *as to the Governor's wife. No one ever thought of taking*
> *a liberty (except a tipsy gentleman from York, and I*
> *am bound to own that my papa never forgave him): he*
> *set the humblest people at once on their ease with him,*
> *and brought down the most arrogant by a grave satiric*
> *way, which made persons exceedingly afraid of him. His*
> *courtesy was not put on like a Sunday suit...They say he*
> *liked to be the first in his company; but what company*
> *was there in which he would not be first?...[He] had a*
> *perfect grace and majesty of deportment, such as I have*
> *never seen in this country.*[16]

To reiterate Gikandi, the aesthetic can never be sutured against or cauterized from the "colonial event," but even more so I propose that the colonial event *is* the aesthetic—that the pleasures, tastes, manners include the juxtaposition. What is pleasing, what is in beautiful form, is the violence. It is a possession; not unpleasant or ugly, it is a desired and valued commodity of an elevated mind, a good character. The virtues espoused cannot be separate from the moments of their production and description.

I don't have to point out the absurdity of the purchased Negroes obeying him with eagerness just because Esmond was good and courteous, humble and of perfect grace, and possessing majesty of deportment. But I want to point out how we are being hailed to enter the fantasy of relations, regularized into the hierarchy. There was an enormous production of this type of fiction/fantasy, all of it sent around the English-speaking world, producing not only the way to live but also the way to imagine and the way to write.

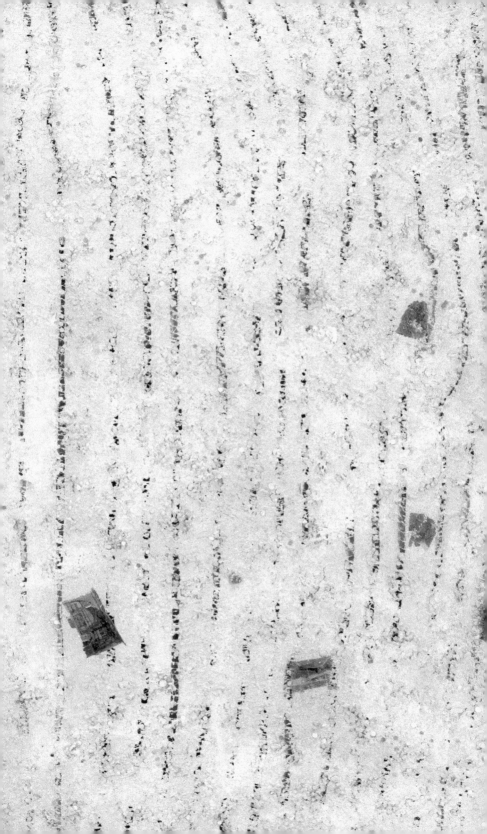

I SPENT THE FIRST seventeen years of my life
consuming this literature, passing through its sentences;
absorbing its form, its structure, and its aesthetic; coming
to know its rules of character, landscape, dialogue, and
so on.

In her essay "Novel and History, Plot and Plantation,"
Sylvia Wynter writes, "we [by which she means plantation
or New World societies] are all, without exception, still
'enchanted,' imprisoned, deformed and schizophrenic in
its bewitched reality."[17]

A narratively constituted imaginary and existence are
repeated, reinforced politically and socially, rewritten in
every novel either as embedded or as dug up to examine
difference or those outside the narrative. If blackness
is one of the categories of this narrative schema, then
it appears as immutable. This narratively constituted
imaginary is a code that considers itself ever changing but
is in fact ever elaborating itself as primary—reconstituting
the same materials in which it is primary, from which it
deals out violence as empathy, violence as love, violence
as the daily enactment of itself. Code and algorithms,
after all, are not neutral or value-free—they are embedded

in, constitutive of, and also produce sets of political and
social relations and, of course, literary ones.

Narrative is not just the simple transportation of
language but of ideas of the self, and ideas of the self that
contain negations of other people. What is it, then, to
adopt or be indoctrinated into these narrative structures,
those ideas, to come to know those ideas as your own,
when you are the negated other people? The intravenous
being, the being administered into being, through the idea
of the universal that is, at the same time, self-negating?

The first strategy of counteracting the toxicity of
colonial narrative may be the counternarrative. I tried
to practise a version of this in my 1988 short story,
"At the Lisbon Plate," when finding no name for the
murdered man in Albert Camus's *L'Étranger/The Outsider*.
I tried to imagine his day, his life before and when he
encounters the colonial anxiety of Camus's Meursault,
a colonial anxiety whose elaboration is the death of the
man on the beach. How Camus un-names the victim
and is unable or unwilling to fill out his life or hear his
voice. And so, in a brief few paragraphs, I attempted in
my early writing life to fill in the register of existence,
since the murdered man's life fell out of the existential
rhetorics of this period in French writing. The murdered
man was outside of existentialism as I was outside of
colonial subjectivity. Even a grand proposition like that
of existentialism cannot contain the existence of the
colonized. "Ahmed. Ahmed. Ahmed," my story begins,
naming the murdered man. "Ahmed came to the beach
with Ousmane to get away...He dropped the bicycle, raced
Ousmane to the water...Ahmed and Ousmane fell into
the sea fully clothed, he washing away the sticky oil of

the bicycle shop, Ousmane drowning his headache."[18]
The story settles Ahmed into his life with his younger
brother, Ousmane, their getaway to the beach, carving a
space away from the penury, the emergencies of the town
and their life. So I had read Camus wanting to enter that
philosophy of existentialism, trying to find some method
of understanding, for a way through, to find a way to that
ideal of humanity, and I found that I had fallen out of the
narrative. But it wasn't inclusion that I wanted. I wanted
to be addressed.

And that brings me back to the *we*—and to *an* and
the. *We* has a certain barbarity to it—a force. It is an
administrative category. Christina Sharpe says, "As one
reads, one always encounters that curious 'we.' That 'we'
constituted with no reference to one's own being—a 'we'
made impossible by 'me.'"[19] To read is to encounter this *we*
at every juncture, even when the word is not invoked, even
in its most benign well-meaning form. I ingested in those
early years of reading the summons and expulsion of *we*.
The desire to enter; the impossibility of entering if...

Within this narrative, what is this reader to be but
nothing, no being, no present, since the reader whose
autobiography is being written is always present—with
no past and no future? A reader is being written with no
character—a reader, inanimate, present as extension of
"the being," "the character." That is to say, this reader
experiences herself as a floating signifier in the narrative,
perpetually escaping from and being captured in
unwanted and unrecognizable signification.

I was influenced of course by Jean Rhys's *Wide Sargasso
Sea*. It is a counternarrative to Charlotte Brontë's *Jane
Eyre*. I imagine Rhys's autobiography of reading was

similar to this one, at least, in some partial way. And probably as an act of correcting the record or animating the inanimate in Brontë's text, Rhys digs up Bertha/ Antoinette to trouble the narratively constituted imaginary. Brontë's *Jane Eyre* was published in the same year, just previous to Thackeray's *Vanity Fair*. In fact, Brontë dedicates the second edition of *Jane Eyre* to Thackeray in admiration of his intellect and wit.

As a child I read Brontë. And later as a university student. *Jane Eyre* is a novel about submission. Confinement and submission—zones of submission. All spaces of the novel are enclosures of female submission—the Reed house, the Lowood orphanage, Rochester's house—zones of submission and indoctrination to familial tyranny, institutional/religious doctrine, and masculinity. The major ethical event is how Jane will resist these zones of submission; the love plot is the next. Necessary to the form of the nineteenth-century novel is the overcoming of (white) female social dissonance through romantic entanglement. The colonial event is hidden in *Jane Eyre*, albeit elaborating itself and growling above in the attic at Thornfield Hall. The hidden violence, the hidden plantation, slavery, in Jamaica, all hidden. I have to think/ extrapolate that everyday middle-class white experience in the nineteenth century must have been familiar with this growling for Brontë to have represented it. A one-paragraph quick summary of this (centuries-long and ongoing) event is performed three-quarters of the way through the novel. Rhys, reading, may have been alert to the hidden woman and the fact that the colonial could not be sutured by the marriage plot.

Imprisoned above in the attic is Bertha Mason and underneath in the drawing rooms and parlours is the gaiety produced by the excesses of the plantation, the violence un-regarded as violence; experienced as power, wealth, and well-being. Thornfield Hall is animated by all of this sublimated violence. It is the expression of violence that everyone is aware of that produces the excitement, the jouissance. The house—filled with guests running to and fro, masquerading, playing charades—is a macabre space. We read:

> everywhere, movement all day long. You could not now traverse the gallery, once so hushed, nor enter the front chambers, once so tenantless, without encountering a smart lady's-maid or a dandy valet.
>
> The kitchen, the butler's pantry, the servants' hall, the entrance hall, were equally alive; and the saloons were only left void and still when the blue sky and halcyon sunshine of the genial spring weather called their occupants out into the grounds...
>
> While Mr. Rochester and the other gentlemen directed these alterations, the ladies were running up and down stairs ringing for their maids. Mrs. Fairfax was summoned to give information respecting the resources of the house in shawls, dresses, draperies of any kind; and certain wardrobes of the third storey were ransacked.[20]

This busyness, this luxury, is produced by the political economy of slavery. As a reader, hailed by extravagance, I did not at first notice the excess, I only experienced the abundance as wonderful—not until later did I experience it as corrupt. The photograph at the beginning of this autobiography was itself a site of submission from which, with time and self-awareness and analysis, I would break free. The meta-data of the photograph demanded affiliation with the protagonist, Jane Eyre. The reader who I was identified herself with Jane—though sidelined and tangential but not disapproving. The reader who I was wished that the woman, the chimera in the attic, would not spoil things.

It is only when Bertha Mason's brother arrives midway through the novel that we get a hint, fleetingly, of the other life that all this luxury is predicated on. This is the first mention of colony, of "some hot country": "Presently the words Jamaica, Kingston, Spanish Town, indicated the West Indies as his residence; and it was with no little surprise I gathered, ere long, that he had there first seen and become acquainted with Mr. Rochester. He spoke of his friend's dislike of the burning heats, the hurricanes, and rainy seasons of that region."[21]

Soon after in the novel, when Mason is stabbed by his sister and Jane is enlisted to nurse him until Rochester gets the doctor, Jane hears

> the snarling, canine noise, and a deep human groan.
> Then my own thoughts worried me. What crime was this
> that lived incarnate in this sequestered mansion, and
> could neither be expelled nor subdued by the owner?—
> what mystery, that broke out now in fire and now in
> blood, at the deadest hours of night? What creature was
> it, that, masked in an ordinary woman's face and shape,
> uttered the voice, now of a mocking demon, and anon of
> a carrion-seeking bird of prey?[22]

Someone like me, reading, finds this a telling paragraph.
Amazingly put. Someone like me reads this snarling and
deep human groan as the unconscious speaking, as the
plantation come to England. This noise—the noise of the
plantation world, the suppressed, the made-mad, the
sequestered—was blackness. This sequestered blackness
would have travelled by boat (like my mother and my aunt
and thousands more later had) as other manifestations of
British psycho-social political economy.

After Rochester hurries the wounded Mason away
before all is discovered, he speaks with Jane outside in the
garden. Listen to the description:

> He strayed down a walk edged with box, with apple trees,
> pear trees, and cherry trees on one side, and a border
> on the other full of all sorts of old-fashioned flowers,
> stocks, sweet-williams, primroses, pansies, mingled with
> southernwood, sweet-briar, and various fragrant herbs.
> They were fresh now as a succession of April showers and
> gleams, followed by a lovely spring morning, could make
> them: the sun was just entering the dappled east, and his
> light illumined the wreathed and dewy orchard trees and
> shone down the quiet walks under them. "Jane, will you
> have a flower?"[23]

It is a most strange turn of narration but completely
understandable since where else could the narrative
go given its colonial project? The trope of the English
garden is employed here—the naturally pristine space.
This appeal to the English natural world—the beauty and
quiet, the less mad, the sane, the rightful order—it is the
justification for all that must be done to maintain the

colonial logic. England and the English psyche remain tranquil and uncontaminated.

But when Jane inherits, it is from her uncle of Madeira: Madeira, which was involved in the slave trade. So far in the novel, Jane has stood relatively outside of the taint, outside of the involvement with plantation/slave capital. But the solution to her full sovereignty is/can only be accomplished by being fully immersed in plantation economics. Madeira once engaged in the production of sugar from sugarcane using enslaved labour from Africa and the Canaries. At the time of the novel and having ended sugar production, for want of resources to exploit, it is now a producer of wine. So, Jane's autonomy, her £25,000 per year so generously shared with her three cousins, is acquired through the same system that Rochester acquires his money. The contentment that she feels and that we are to feel for her is riven with violence.

Jean Rhys takes care of Rochester's brief account (one or two paragraphs in Brontë's *Jane Eyre*) of his involvement with Bertha Mason, whose real name we come to know is Antoinette, her name changed by Rochester in an act of possession and right to name. In an act of counternarration, Rhys un-names Rochester. While Rhys exposes the political economy of slave-holding and the marriage arrangement/ plot as buttressing these relations, she leaves unopened the fantasy of the enslaved's love for the master. The figure of Christophine is unexplainable as protector and mother figure to Antoinette and her mother. A Black woman formerly enslaved by Antoinette's family is presented as Antoinette's defender and protector against Rochester. A reader like me observes this. Christophine confronts Rochester about his true motives. "You think you fool me?" she asks him. "You want her money but you don't want her...You do that for money? But you wicked like Satan self!"[24] Christophine in the years since emancipation and Antoinette's growing-up has been imprisoned for being an Obeah woman and healer—a status crime of colonial times since these women were usually at the forefront of fomenting rebellion. So, while Rhys presents the figure of Christophine as a powerful one, her love and caring for Antoinette is inexplicable— and only explicable within the same narrative construction as *Jane Eyre*—the underside of that violence is the narrative of mutual love, filial love as operating outside of violence. *Wide Sargasso Sea* also has these Black figures (as opposed to people) who populate the text, as crowd or townsfolk, whose actions and movements and whisperings are unexplainable, surreptitious, belligerent, without explanation, and therefore purely malevolent. (Malevolent as opposed to rebellious—or desirous of taking and making freedom.) *Wide Sargasso Sea* is told in two voices, Antoinette's and Rochester's, there could just as easily have been three voices. And the lack of a third voice is structurally unaccountable—except for that logic.

If one is a reader like me, one notices these things. One wants to completely embrace *Wide Sargasso Sea*, strangely as this same reader wanted to embrace *Jane Eyre* and had. Such a reader ignores the misgivings, or rather reads with a set of aches, like forming a callus at each reading. Such a reader has a mindbox inside of a mindbox inside of a mindbox and so on.

John Keene's *Counternarratives*, a book of short stories and novellas, makes explicit the act of blowing life into the world of coloniality. In his short story "Rivers," in the section of the book called "Counternarratives," Keene offers a counter to Mark Twain's *Huckleberry Finn*. At the centre of this story is James Rivers, whom we meet after the Civil War. James Rivers is and is not the Jim of Twain's book. Rivers recounts the time when a reporter who is supposed to interview him about "the war and his service in it" instead asks him a question about "that boy" (Huck Finn), whom he has seen only twice in the intervening forty years. The story begins: "What I'd like to hear about, the reporter starts in, is the time you and that little boy... and I silence again with a turn of my head thinking to myself."[25] And what follows is a partial list of the places where he was and battles he participated in in what he names "the first great war for *our* freedom."[26] This *our*, italicized in Keene's text, is very clear—this *our* references Black freedom, and it stands counter to that violent *we* I spoke of earlier.

Both the reporter's question, and its narrative demand, want to return Rivers to a time and place he has worked to forget—or, perhaps more to the point, to return him to a point that is not the point of his life. The reporter's question would take him back to Twain's narrative in which the white boy/man and not James Rivers is at the centre, but Rivers has his own narrative. And Keene gives us James Rivers's narrative at first, by way of a face turned away in refusal and then by way of a remembered encounter in which the necessary dissimulation, evidenced in the grammar of the past conditional, is on the page: "I silence him thinking to myself, I thought to say, I thought to say, I thought to tell the boy, I thought to say, I thought to say, I thought to recount, I thought to narrate."[27] The body of the story tells of River's life, not of his performance in a picaresque *about* a white boy.

These works by Rhys and Keene, and my small contribution of "At the Lisbon Plate," take linear mapping as a strategy—of unearthing, unlayering, and revealing. Using, perhaps, the same structure of storytelling—mirroring and correcting or mirroring to correct. My concern is if that is enough for decentring. What if one ignores entirely that which has been produced so far as it exists along a colonial schema? A schema that makes the narrative of empire addressable always, that leaves intact the history and method of colonial narrativizing, and presumes a unitary subject of narrative production?

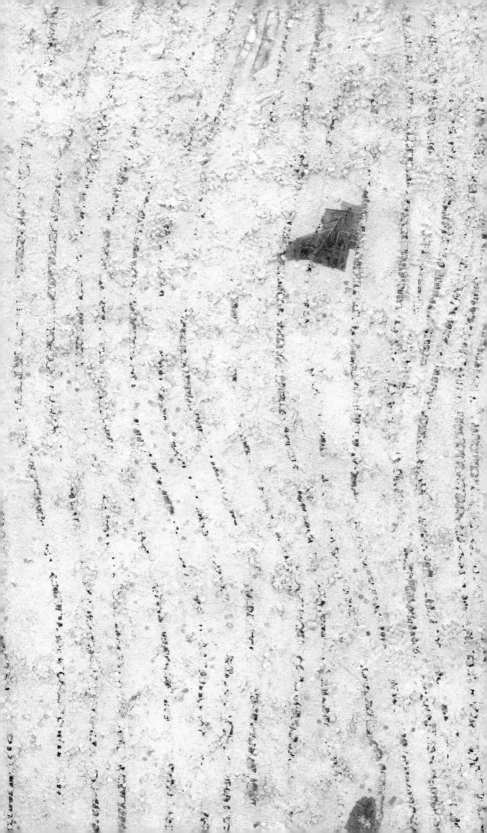

THE SECOND STRATEGY. What if one were to
completely ignore narrative demands' synergies between
the social arrangements and meta-story? We occupy a
certain position in the Western modern so the meta-
story and all ancillary stories must be in synergy; and
these ancillary stories are also produced by Black people.
There is then the difficult work of narrativizing the life of
Black people, as that life sits at a cardinal coordinate of
capital and white power, is located in the racist schema
that capital and white power describe. The task of the
writer, whether of fiction or non-fiction, or of casual or
bureaucratic texts, is to narrate our own consciousnesses,
to describe a Black life in the register of the social and
the political and not in the register of pathologies or the
pathological. I am thinking here of Saidiya Hartman's
majestic book, *Wayward Lives, Beautiful Experiments:
Intimate Histories of Social Upheaval*, in which she refuses
the forms of bureaucratic writing—state writing—that
narrativize Black people into multiple forms and states of
incarceration.

Gwendolyn Brooks's *Maud Martha* is one such example
in fiction—a narrative attending to its own expression,

attending to describing its consciousness. Here in *Maud Martha* is a consciousness unimpeded by the demand to locate itself as adjacent to a spectator who wishes to dislocate that consciousness or make it inanimate and tangential. The mindbox opens in the reader. Brooks arranges an ordinary life without a spectator who is invested in violence as the only mode of, or code for, referencing that life:

> Up the street, mixed in the wind, blew the children, and turned the corner onto the brownish red brick school court. It was wonderful. Bits of pink of blue, white yellow, green, purple, brown, black, carried by jerky little stems of brown or yellow or brown-black, blew by the unhandsome gray and decay of the double-apartment buildings, past the little plots of dirt and scanty grass...There were lives in the buildings. Past the tiny lives the children blew.[28]

The children in her description may be very similar to the four children of the photograph at Mr. Wong's studio. Their disarray as yet unattended by the violence of colonial pedagogy. Violence surely hovers and presages their presence, but the alertness of their presence and their desires are the foregrounded, crucial details. Brooks's narrator *sees* them. There is a sense in which the children in Mr. Wong's photograph escape the reference of colony—they have yet to be collected. It is recorded in their discombobulation, their fear, their panic, their crying, their distance—signs of their sovereignty—their resistance to being gathered.

The beauty of *Maud Martha* is that it assumes this sovereign point of view, and it is in this *address* that it locates its protagonist and the world. Maud Martha's ruminations, too, occupy the central philosophical ground, not the partial or adjunct. Brooks writes:

> *People have to choose something decently constant to depend on, thought Maud Martha. People must have something to lean on. But the love of a single person was not enough. Not only was personal love itself, however good, a thing that varied from week to week, from second to second, but the parties to it were likely, for example, to die, any minute, or otherwise be parted, or destroyed... Could be nature, which had a seed, or root, or an element (what do you want to call it) of constancy, under all that system of change. Of course, to say "system" at all implied arrangement, and therefore some order of constancy.*[29]

Brooks suggests another *we* entirely, one that beckons a reader, such as me, with familiarity; with a proposition; an invitation to construct the narrative's coherence without requiring the presumption of an abject location. It is a *we* into which this reader might be gathered.

Palace of the Peacock by Wilson Harris is another narrative that requires no callus to withstand or elide the violence of one's absent presence. For me, it is an origin novel in terms of its subject as well as its method. It practises what Édouard Glissant calls opacity (as does Brooks's *Maud Martha*, come to think of it). The event is the event of the colonial, but all elements, all characters, are present and in flux.

In *Palace of the Peacock*, the I narrator—who is singular, dual, and multiple—writes:

> "In fact I belong already. [...] Is it a mystery of language
> and address?" [...] I searched for words with a sudden
> terrible rage at the difficulty I experienced... "it's an
> inapprehension of substance," I blurted out, "an actual
> fear..fear of life...fear of the substance of life, fear of the
> substance of the folk, a cannibal blind fear in oneself.
> Put it how you like," I cried, "it's fear of acknowledging
> the true substance of life. [...] And somebody," I declared,
> "must demonstrate the unity of being, and show..."
> I had grown violent and emphatic... "that fear is nothing
> but a dream and an appearance...even death..." I stopped
> abruptly.[30]

The tale is of a journey into the forests of Guyana with
all the pre- and post-Columbian actors. In the structure
of the novel, you are never fully aware of its purpose or
assured of its outcome. It is a reckoning with coloniality.
And since coloniality seeks to order its human objects
particular ways, including through narration and
narrative style, then Harris's novel refuses that narration,
and narrative style, for the more complex one that exists.
He uses a multifocal lens, multiple and shifting points
of view—as if attempting to make the reader see, hear,
everyone at once and to read everything at once. Kenneth
Ramchand points out that Harris disliked "the novel
of persuasion" and felt that "since the 'medium' has
been conditioned by previous use and framed by ruling
ideologies, there has to be an assault upon the medium
including not only the form of the novel but also the
premises about language that are inscribed in the novel."[31]

At Atocha Train Station in Madrid one summer, every
move my companion and I make in the line to the ticket

counter is interrupted by whites wishing to cross to the
other side of the room. No matter how the line moves,
how much closer to the wicket we advance, we are located
and used, by whites crossing the room, as the sign for
space.

In *Caribbean Discourse*, Édouard Glissant writes about
the importance of form when thinking about the ghosts
of colonialism, which reverberates into the present and
future. For him, narrative "implode[s] in us in clumps"
and we are "transported [to] fields of oblivion where we
must, with difficulty and pain, put it all back together."[32]

If structures of sociality derived from the colonial
moment pursue us and are anathema to our living, and if
such structures include narration and narrative style,
then a rethinking of these forms of address is necessary—
I would say urgent, as urgent as the overturning of that
sociality.

IN JANE EYRE, when Mr. Brocklehurst exhorts Miss
Temple at Lowood orphanage—"Oh, madam, when you
put bread and cheese, instead of burnt porridge, into
these children's mouths, you may indeed feed their vile
bodies, but you little think how you starve their immortal
souls!"[33]—it is reminiscent of the doctrine of all my
primary school teachers, beginning with Miss Greenidge's
Dame School when I was three years old. It strikes me
that they may have read and lived by this and that I
may have been one of those children, though not in an
orphanage, but yet in the great storeroom/training school
of British imperialism.

The girl in the photograph—who is and is not me, who
is and is not the reader—is still making the photograph.
Her sisters and her cousin around her are also making
their own photographs, despite her earlier assumption
that it is she who is most active in the photograph. That
is the beauty of a photograph. The succeeding hours
outside the photography studio still have not happened—
Vanity Fair has not been read; Jane Eyre has not been read.
The tensions in the photograph, the set of colonial and
other relations that bring all into the studio, may also be

arranged toward or in another narrative. The photograph is previous. The aunt may have gone back to Tenerife. Over the phone in the present, Tenerife is so vivid in her recollection as a site of beauty and longing. The activity, the haste (of the studio—the brown curtain, the flowered floor); the frame, which one has to adjust oneself to or refuse, something like an autobiography, is only becoming present; but the tensions of the frame suggest a small resistance, if not by the girl who is alleged to be me, then to the autobiography of the composed subject. The disarray of the participants; their permeability and liminality, which are the only possessions they have at the moment of taking the photograph—their nothing-yet future and their still-unknown (to themselves) past—all this can still become. The girl who is supposed to be me is insisting on a photograph, an autobiography of some kind. She does not yet understand (maybe she only glimpses) the full-on violence of narrative. She is trying to be, to centre the girls in the photograph, to find the new medium.

NOTES

1. Samuel Selvon, *The Lonely Londoners* (London: Penguin Books, 2006), 1. First published 1956.
2. C.L.R. James, *Beyond a Boundary* (New York: Pantheon, 1963), 47.
3. James, *Beyond a Boundary*, 47.
4. James, *Beyond a Boundary*, 48.
5. James, *Beyond a Boundary*, 48.
6. James, *Beyond a Boundary*, 40–41.
7. James, *Beyond a Boundary*, 41–42.
8. Lisa Lowe, *The Intimacies of Four Continents* (Durham, NC: Duke University Press, 2015), 81.
9. William Makepeace Thackeray, *Vanity Fair* (Mineola, NY: Dover Thrift Editions, 2016), 14. First published 1848.
10. Thackeray, *Vanity Fair*, 7.
11. Thackeray, *Vanity Fair*, 3.
12. Edward Said, *Culture and Imperialism* (New York: Vintage, 1994), 62.
13. William Makepeace Thackeray, *The History of Henry Esmond, Esq.* (Harmondsworth: Penguin, 1970), 37. First published 1852.
14. Simon Gikandi, "Aesthetic Reflection and the Colonial Event: The Work of Art in the Age of Slavery," *Journal of the International Institute* 4, no. 3 (Spring/Summer 1997): 12.
15. Thackeray, *The History of Henry Esmond, Esq.*, 38.
16. Thackeray, *The History of Henry Esmond, Esq.*, 40.

17. Sylvia Wynter, "Novel and History, Plot and Plantation," *Savacou* 5 (1971): 95.

18. Dionne Brand, "At the Lisbon Plate," in *Sans Souci, and Other Stories* (Toronto: Williams-Wallace, 1988), 113.

19. Christina Sharpe, personal communication, October 2018.

20. Charlotte Brontë, *Jane Eyre* (London: Service and Patton, 1897), 181. First published 1847.

21. Brontë, *Jane Eyre*, 191.

22. Brontë, *Jane Eyre*, 210.

23. Brontë, *Jane Eyre*, 215.

24. Jean Rhys, *Wide Sargasso Sea* (New York: W.W. Norton & Company, 2016), 161. First published in 1966.

25. John Keene, "Rivers," in *Counternarratives* (New York: Directions, 2015), 219.

26. Keene, "Rivers," 219.

27. Keene, "Rivers," 222–25.

28. Gwendolyn Brooks, *Maud Martha* (Chicago: Third World Press, 1991), 146.

29. Brooks, *Maud Martha*, 242–43.

30. Wilson Harris, *Palace of the Peacock* (London: Faber and Faber, 2013), loc 526–31, Kindle. First published 1966.

31. Kenneth Ramchand, Afterword to *Palace of the Peacock*, loc 1451, Kindle.

32. Édouard Glissant, *Caribbean Discourse: Selected Essays* (Charlottesville: University of Virginia Press, 1996), 145.

33. Brontë, *Jane Eyre*, 63.

CLC KREISEL LECTURE SERIES